I am
UNIQUE

Copyright © 2021 Akudo U Ehirim All rights reserved.
First paperback edition printed 2021 in the
United Kingdom
A catalogue record for this book is available from
the British Library.
ISBN 978-1-913455-31-6
No part of this book shall be reproduced or transmitted in
any form or by any means,
electronic or mechanical, including photocopying,
recording, or by any information retrieval
system without written permission of the publisher.
Published by Scribblecity Publications
Printed in Great Britain
Although every precaution has been taken in the
preparation of this book, the publisher and
author assume no responsibility for errors or omissions.
Neither is any liability assumed for
damages resulting from the use of this information
contained herein.
Illustrated by Omerbia Aja-Nwachuku.

Dedicated to the children of the world
who are special and unique in their own way.

I may be **disabled** or **handicapped**

Deaf   Blind

Crippled   Speechless (dumb)

BUt I am still **special**

I may be a **different** size

Big   Small

Yellow   Brown

But I am still **special**

I may be a **different** race

African American   Caucasian

I may be in a **different** mood

I may **have** a **different** pet

Cat   Dog

Fish   Bird

BUT I am still special

I may **have** a **different** type of **hair**

Long hair

Short hair

I may **have** a **different** mommy

Old mom   Young mom

But I am still special

I may *live* in a **different** place

House   Apartment

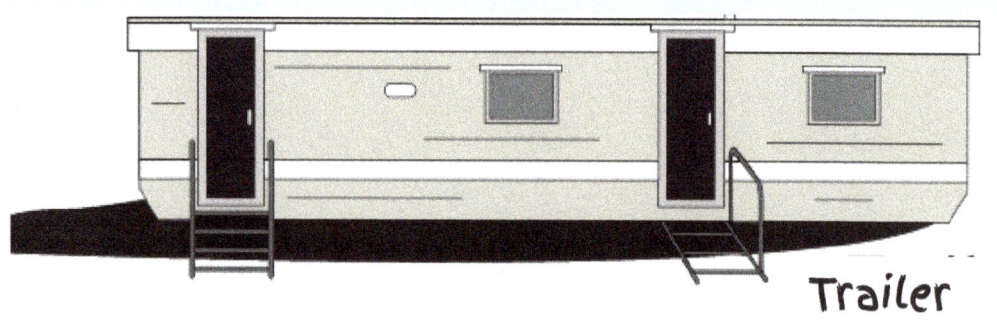

Trailer

Bungalow

But I am still **special**

I may *live* with **two** parents

Mommy and Daddy

Or I may **live** with **one** parent

Daddy　　or　　Mommy

Being **different** is being **special**, and being special is being **unique**.

I am a **beautiful, handsome** and **unique** person, and I am **proud** of who I am.

Are **YOU**?

www.ingramcontent.com/pod-product-compliance
Lightning Source LLC
Chambersburg PA
CBHW042000080526
44588CB00021B/2820